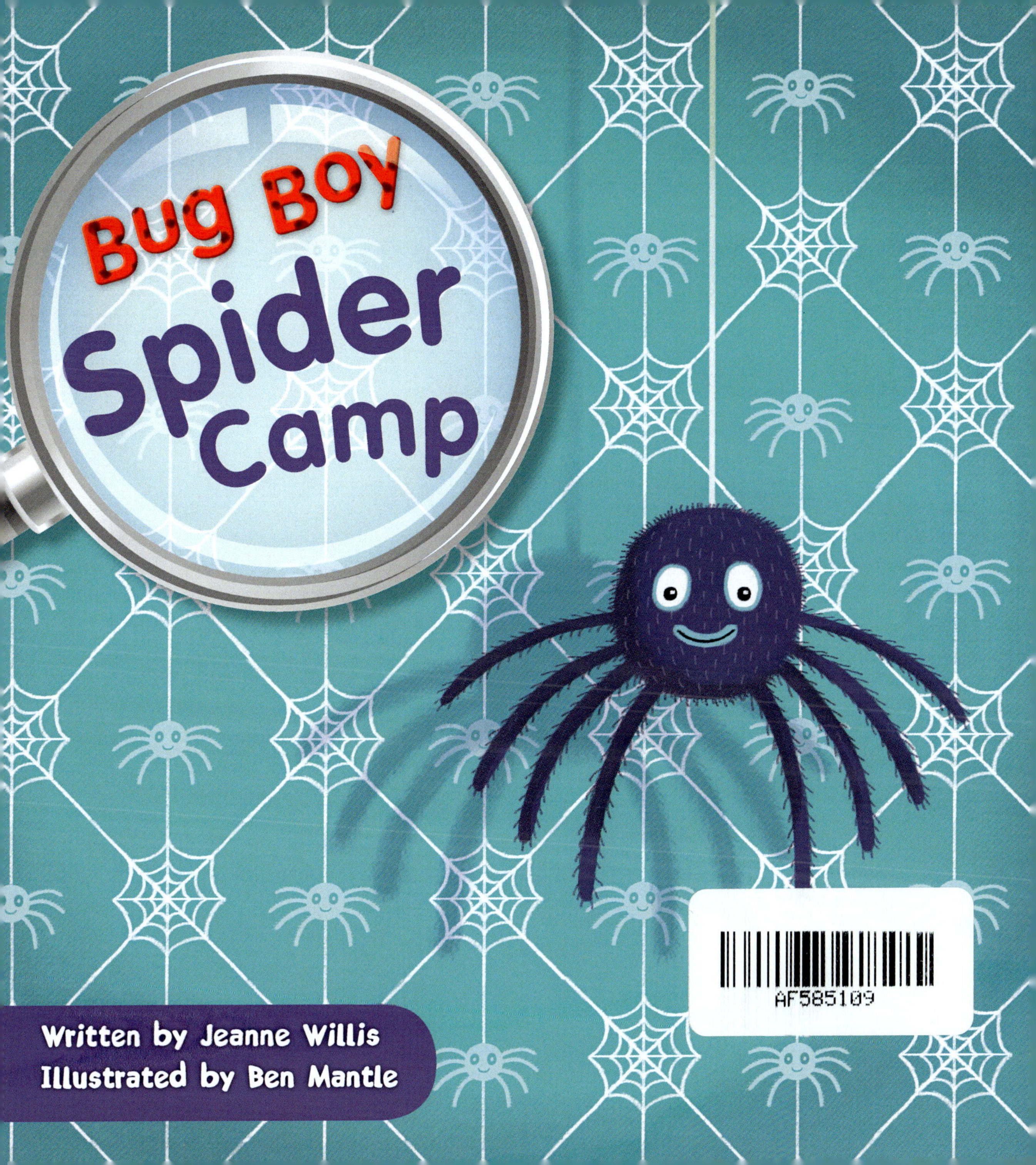
Bug Boy
Spider Camp
AF585109
Written by Jeanne Willis
Illustrated by Ben Mantle

Dan had lots of bugs.

He had a bug zoo!

One day, there was a **big** spider.

Dan put the spider in a jar.
"This is Tom," he said.

“Come on, Dan,” said Dad.
“We are going camping.”

“Come on, Tom,” said Dan.
“You are going camping, too.”

It was a long trip in the car.
Emma got cross with Dan.

“I will **not** sleep in Dan’s tent!” said Emma.

Emma went in the big tent.

Dan was in his little tent.
He let Tom out of the jar.

In the night, Emma came to Dan's tent.
"Let me in!" she said.
"Dad is snoring!"

"No! Tom is in here.
You will **not** like him," said Dan.
But Emma got into the tent.

Tom fell on her!
"**Yuck!**" said Emma.

Plop!

"Goodnight, Tom!" said Dan.